The Ultimate Tornado Book For Kids

Rodney Harris

Foreword

When I was a kid growing up in Oklahoma, I remember lying in bed at night listening to the sound of thunder roll across the sky. Sometimes, the house would shake just a little, the windows would rattle, and I'd sneak out of my room to check the radar on the old weather TV in the living room. I was fascinated—scared, yes—but also totally captivated by the power and mystery of storms.

That childhood curiosity never left me. It's what led me to study weather, chase storms, and eventually write this book. **Tornadoes are some of the most powerful and awe-inspiring forces on Earth**, and while they can be dangerous, they're also incredible examples of nature's power at work. My goal with this book is simple: to make you smarter, safer, and more amazed than ever before by what tornadoes can do.

This book is for every curious kid who's ever looked up at a swirling sky and wondered what's going on up there. It's for the readers who love adventure, crave cool science facts, and want to understand how tornadoes form, how they're tracked, and how to stay safe when they appear. It's also for the future meteorologists, storm chasers, engineers, and community helpers who are just beginning their journey into the world of weather.

Inside these chapters, you'll find **stories, science, and even hands-on activities** that will help you explore tornadoes from every angle—how they're born, how we study them, how they impact people and animals, and how they've shown up in books, movies, and myths.

Most of all, I hope this book makes you feel empowered. When we understand storms, we don't have to be afraid—we can be prepared.

So grab your flashlight, your curiosity, and your sense of wonder. There's a storm coming… and it's going to be awesome.

Stay safe and stay curious,
Rodney Harris

Chapter 1: What Is a Tornado?

Defining a Tornado

Imagine a giant spinning column of air that drops down from a thunderstorm and touches the ground, swirling with incredible power—that's a tornado! Tornadoes are one of nature's most intense and mysterious weather events. They may look like something out of a movie, but they're very real and can do a lot of damage in just a few minutes.

A tornado forms when warm, moist air near the ground meets cold, dry air higher in the sky. When these two air masses collide, they can create strong thunderstorms. If wind conditions are just right, those thunderstorms can begin to rotate, and a tornado might form. The tornado spins violently in a tight column, often shaped like a cone or tube, and moves across the land.

Tornadoes can last just a few seconds or go on for more than an hour. They can be small and skinny or wide enough to stretch a mile across! Some tornadoes move slowly, while others zip along at speeds over 50 miles per hour. And even though they're usually visible as dark, swirling funnels, some are hard to see—especially if it's dark or raining heavily.

Different Names for Tornadoes

You may have heard different names used to describe tornadoes, like *twisters* or *cyclones*. While people often use these words to mean the same thing, there are actually some differences:

- **Twister**: This is a common nickname for a tornado, especially in movies or books. It refers to how the tornado twists through the air.

- **Whirlwind**: This term can describe any spinning column of air, but it's usually used for smaller wind events, like dust devils. A tornado is a powerful type of whirlwind.

- **Cyclone**: Here's where it gets tricky. In the United States, a cyclone often refers to a large storm system like a hurricane or a low-pressure area with rotating winds. However, in some countries like Australia and India, people call tornadoes "cyclones" too. That can be confusing, so meteorologists try to use the word "tornado" when they mean the twisting storm that touches the ground.

So, while these names sometimes overlap, *tornado* is the most specific and scientific term to describe the storm we're talking about in this book.

Parts of a Tornado

Even though a tornado might look like one big spinning cloud, it's made up of several parts. Understanding what each part does can help you picture how powerful and complicated these storms really are.

- **Funnel Cloud**: This is the visible part of the tornado that extends from the base of a thunderstorm. It looks like a cone or rope hanging from the sky. A funnel cloud becomes a tornado when it touches the ground.

- **Vortex**: This is the central part of the tornado where air is rotating the fastest. It's invisible, but it's what gives a tornado its intense spin.

- **Debris Cloud**: When a tornado reaches the ground, it picks up dust, dirt, leaves, and even objects like fences, tree branches, and pieces of buildings. This swirling mess is the debris cloud, and it often surrounds the funnel.

- **Wall Cloud**: This is a larger, darker cloud that hangs lower than the rest of the thunderstorm. Tornadoes often form underneath wall clouds.

Some tornadoes even have **multiple vortices**, which means smaller tornadoes spin around the main one, like a spinning top surrounded by little dancers. These can cause even more damage because they hit more places in a short time.

Tornado vs. Other Storms

Tornadoes are often confused with other big storms, but they're quite different from hurricanes, cyclones, and thunderstorms.

- **Tornado vs. Hurricane**: A tornado is a small, narrow column of fast-spinning air that forms during a thunderstorm and touches the ground. A hurricane, on the other hand, is a giant storm system that forms over warm ocean water and can stretch hundreds of miles across. Hurricanes last for days, while tornadoes usually last minutes.

- **Tornado vs. Cyclone**: In the U.S., "cyclone" is used for low-pressure weather systems with rotating winds, not tornadoes. But in some other countries, cyclone means the same thing as a hurricane—or sometimes even a tornado!

- **Tornado vs. Thunderstorm**: Tornadoes are born inside powerful thunderstorms, but not all thunderstorms create tornadoes. Thunderstorms have lightning, thunder, rain, and wind, but they don't always spin.

- **Tornado vs. Dust Devil**: Dust devils are tiny whirlwinds that form on hot, sunny days. They're harmless compared to tornadoes and usually spin in open areas like parking lots or deserts.

So while these storms may all involve strong winds and clouds, tornadoes are unique for their size, shape, and super-speedy rotation.

Tornado Facts to Blow You Away

Tornadoes aren't just fascinating—they're full of wild facts and mind-blowing records that show just how extreme they can be. Here are some cool tornado facts kids love:

- The fastest wind speed ever recorded in a tornado was **302 miles per hour** in the 1999 Bridge Creek–Moore tornado in Oklahoma.

- The **Tri-State Tornado of 1925** traveled across three states—Missouri, Illinois, and Indiana—and was the deadliest in U.S. history, killing 695 people.

- The widest tornado ever recorded was over **2.6 miles wide**! It happened near El Reno, Oklahoma in 2013.

- Tornadoes have been known to pick up **cars, cows, and even entire houses** and toss them hundreds of feet.

- A tornado once carried a **postcard 200 miles** away, and it was later found and returned to its owner!

- **Waterspouts** are tornadoes that form over water. They look beautiful but can still be dangerous to boats and people.

- On average, the United States sees **more than 1,000 tornadoes a year**—more than any other country.

Tornadoes may be scary, but they're also some of nature's most powerful and awe-inspiring forces. Now that you know what a tornado is and how it works, you're ready to dive deeper into the science behind them. The next chapter will take you inside the storm to discover how tornadoes are born from the perfect mix of air, wind, and weather.

Chapter 2: How Tornadoes Are Born

The Perfect Storm: Conditions Needed for Tornado Formation

Tornadoes don't just pop up out of nowhere—they require a perfect mix of ingredients in the atmosphere to form. These ingredients include warm, moist air near the ground, cold, dry air higher up in the sky, and strong winds blowing in different directions. When these pieces come together, they can create a powerful thunderstorm capable of spinning up a tornado.

Think of it like baking a cake. If you leave out a key ingredient, your cake won't turn out right. The same goes for tornadoes. You need:

- **Warm, moist air** from the Gulf of Mexico (or other warm bodies of water)
- **Cool, dry air** from Canada or the Rocky Mountains
- **Wind shear**, which means the wind is blowing in different directions or speeds at different heights
- A **trigger**, like a cold front or dry line, to get the air moving upward

When these forces meet, they can produce towering thunderclouds that stretch miles into the sky. And if the winds are just right, those clouds can start to spin. That's when tornado trouble begins.

Inside a Thunderstorm: How Thunderstorms Develop and Connect to Tornadoes

Before a tornado can form, a thunderstorm must form first. A thunderstorm is created when warm air at the surface rises and meets cooler air above. As the warm air rises, it cools and condenses into clouds. If enough warm air keeps rising, the clouds grow taller and taller, sometimes reaching over 50,000 feet high.

Thunderstorms go through three main stages:

1. **Cumulus Stage**: Warm air rises and forms puffy clouds.
2. **Mature Stage**: The storm is full-grown, with heavy rain, lightning, thunder, and possibly hail.
3. **Dissipating Stage**: The storm begins to lose energy and fall apart.

Tornadoes usually form during the mature stage, when the storm is strongest. If winds within the thunderstorm begin to rotate horizontally and then tilt upward, that rotation can become a spinning funnel cloud. If that funnel touches the ground, it becomes a tornado.

Not all thunderstorms produce tornadoes. Most are just loud and rainy. But some powerful storms have the special conditions needed to spin—and that's when things get serious.

Updrafts, Downdrafts, and Wind Shear: How Wind Plays a Role

Wind is one of the most important ingredients in tornado formation. But it's not just about how strong the wind is—it's about how the wind moves in different parts of the storm.

- **Updrafts** are columns of warm air that rise into the sky. These keep a thunderstorm alive and growing.

- **Downdrafts** are cooler winds that blow downward from the storm, helping push rain and hail toward the ground.

- **Wind shear** happens when the wind changes direction or speed with height. For example, it might blow from the south at the ground but from the west up high.

Wind shear can cause the rising air in a thunderstorm to begin spinning. Imagine placing your hand flat on a spinning basketball and tilting it—suddenly the spin changes direction. In a thunderstorm, tilting wind shear can turn horizontal spin into vertical rotation. That's what helps a funnel cloud form.

If the updraft is strong enough to stretch and tighten that rotation, the spin becomes faster and more focused. This tight spin is what forms the center of a tornado.

Supercells: The Tornado Factories

While many thunderstorms look the same, one type is especially dangerous when it comes to producing tornadoes. These are called **supercells**.

A supercell is a special kind of thunderstorm with a rotating core called a **mesocyclone**. This rotation is the key difference between supercells and regular storms. Mesocyclones form when wind shear and strong updrafts combine in just the right way.

Inside a supercell, winds twist and turn in all directions. This rotation can stretch into a funnel cloud, and if it drops to the ground, it becomes a tornado. Not all supercells produce tornadoes, but almost all strong, long-lasting tornadoes come from supercells.

Supercells can last for hours and travel for hundreds of miles. They often bring hail, heavy rain, lightning, and destructive winds—even if they don't produce a tornado. Meteorologists watch supercells closely because they are the number-one source of the most violent tornadoes.

Tracking the Lifecycle of a Tornado: From Funnel Cloud to Dissipation

Tornadoes may be short-lived compared to other storms, but they go through their own life cycle. Here's how a tornado typically forms, grows, and fades away:

1. **Funnel Cloud Stage**: Rotation begins in the storm and a funnel cloud forms, hanging down from the cloud base. It hasn't touched the ground yet, so it's not officially a tornado.

2. **Touchdown Stage**: The funnel cloud reaches the ground and begins picking up dirt and debris. This is

when it becomes a tornado.

3. **Mature Stage**: The tornado is at its strongest. It may grow wider, become darker with debris, and move across the land, causing damage.

4. **Shrinking Stage**: The tornado begins to weaken. It may become thinner, rope-like, and wobble as it loses strength.

5. **Dissipation Stage**: The tornado lifts off the ground and disappears back into the cloud. The storm may still continue for a while, but the tornado is gone.

Sometimes, a storm will produce **more than one tornado**, either at the same time or one after the other. This is called a **tornado outbreak**. These events can be especially dangerous because they affect large areas with little time to recover between storms.

Understanding how tornadoes are born helps scientists and storm spotters know when conditions are right for dangerous weather. From the mixing of warm and cold air to the wild spinning of a supercell, every step in the process plays a role in forming these powerful storms. Now that you know how a tornado gets its start, you're ready to learn about just how powerful it can become.

Chapter 3: The Power of the Wind

The Enhanced Fujita Scale: EF0 to EF5 Explained in Kid-Friendly Terms

When a tornado rips through a town or countryside, one of the first things scientists want to figure out is how strong it was. But since it's hard to stick a wind gauge in the middle of a tornado, meteorologists use a special system called the **Enhanced Fujita Scale**, or **EF Scale** for short.

This scale doesn't measure the wind directly. Instead, it looks at the damage the tornado caused—like roofs being torn off houses, trees being uprooted, or buildings completely destroyed—and estimates how fast the wind must have been.

The scale goes from EF0 to EF5:

- **EF0** (65–85 mph): Light damage. Might break small tree branches or peel shingles off a roof.

- **EF1** (86–110 mph): Moderate damage. Mobile homes may be pushed off their foundations, and cars can be moved.

- **EF2** (111–135 mph): Considerable damage. Roofs ripped off homes, large trees uprooted.

- **EF3** (136–165 mph): Severe damage. Entire stories of homes can be destroyed, trains overturned.

- **EF4** (166–200 mph): Devastating damage. Well-built homes leveled, cars thrown through the air.

- **EF5** (Over 200 mph): Incredible damage. Strong homes turned to rubble, steel-reinforced buildings severely damaged.

EF5 tornadoes are extremely rare, but when they hit, the destruction is beyond belief. Most tornadoes in the U.S. are EF0 or EF1, but it's always important to take every tornado warning seriously, no matter how strong it might seem.

What Can the Wind Do?: Real Examples of Tornado Destruction

Tornado winds may be invisible, but they're strong enough to move things that weigh thousands of pounds. Here are just a few jaw-dropping examples of what tornadoes have done:

- A tornado in **El Reno, Oklahoma** in 2013 tossed a 10-ton oil tanker truck like a toy, flinging it hundreds of feet.

- During the **Joplin, Missouri tornado in 2011**, entire blocks of homes were leveled, and even hospitals and schools were torn apart.

- In **Greensburg, Kansas**, an EF5 tornado destroyed 95% of the town in just minutes.

- In one case, a piece of straw was found stuck straight through a tree—driven in by the force of the wind.

Tornado winds don't just destroy buildings. They can rip up pavement, twist metal beams, and strip bark off trees. They can lift cars, trucks, and even trains off the ground. And sometimes, they scatter debris so far that pieces of buildings are found miles away.

Wind Speeds That Wow: Comparing Tornado Winds to Jet Planes and Race Cars

It's hard to imagine just how fast tornado winds can be. Let's compare them to things you might be more familiar with:

- A professional race car might travel at about **200 miles per hour**—fast, but still within the range of a tornado.
- Commercial jets take off at about **150–180 mph**. Some tornadoes have wind speeds faster than that.
- The strongest tornado winds ever recorded reached over **300 mph**—faster than any car, faster than most planes, and definitely faster than any roller coaster.

Here's a fun comparison: if you stood outside in an EF5 tornado (which you should *never* do!), it would feel like being hit by a wall of air traveling faster than a speeding bullet train.

Tornadoes may be small compared to hurricanes, but the wind inside a tornado is the fastest wind on Earth.

Why Not All Tornadoes Are the Same: Differences in Size, Speed, and Lifespan

Tornadoes come in all shapes and sizes, and no two are exactly alike. Some are thin and ropy, while others are wide and look like giant wedges.

Size:

- A small tornado might be just **10 yards wide**—narrower than a school bus.
- A massive tornado, like the **El Reno tornado**, can grow over **2.6 miles wide**—wider than 40 football fields.

Speed:

- Some tornadoes crawl along at just **10 mph**, while others race across the land at **70 mph** or more.
- The faster they move, the harder they are to avoid, which is why quick warnings are so important.

Lifespan:

- Some tornadoes touch down for only a few seconds and cause little damage.
- Others can last over an hour and carve paths over **100 miles** long.

There are even rare cases of **multiple-vortex tornadoes**, where smaller "mini-tornadoes" swirl around the main funnel, creating even more damage in more places at once.

Because tornadoes vary so much, scientists have to look at each one carefully to figure out how dangerous it was—and to improve how we prepare for the next one.

Twister Trivia: Surprising Wind-Related Facts

Tornadoes aren't just powerful—they're full of surprising secrets. Here are some amazing wind-related tornado facts:

- The United States gets more tornadoes than any other country—**over 1,000 each year**.
- The **Tri-State Tornado** in 1925 stayed on the ground for **219 miles**, the longest ever recorded.
- Tornadoes can spin either **clockwise or counterclockwise**, but most in the U.S. rotate counterclockwise.
- Some tornadoes are so quiet you wouldn't hear them coming, while others sound like **freight trains**.
- A tornado once blew a **metal sign through a wall**—with the edges bent like paper.
- A tornado near **Parker, Colorado** once sucked water from a pond, raining frogs and fish down on the nearby area.

- Wind from an EF4 tornado is strong enough to **snap a tree like a toothpick** or send a mattress flying through the air like a frisbee.

Tornado winds may be invisible, but they leave a powerful mark on everything they touch. Whether it's tossing trucks, flattening buildings, or sending everyday objects flying through the air, the force of a tornado is something to respect and study. As we move forward, we'll learn where these mighty storms hit the most—and how people prepare for them across the globe.

Chapter 4: Tornado Alley and Beyond

Where Is Tornado Alley?: States and Regions Most at Risk

When people think of tornadoes, they often picture the central United States—flat land, wide skies, and spinning funnels stretching down from the clouds. That's because this part of the country is known as **Tornado Alley**, the region where tornadoes happen more often than almost anywhere else on Earth.

Tornado Alley isn't an official place with borders, but meteorologists use the term to describe a wide area across the central U.S. where the conditions for tornadoes are just right. The main states often included in Tornado Alley are:

- **Texas**
- **Oklahoma**
- **Kansas**
- **Nebraska**
- **South Dakota**
- **Missouri**
- **Iowa**

Some people also include parts of Colorado, New Mexico, and Arkansas. Texas alone sees more tornadoes than any other state—hundreds each year!

The reason Tornado Alley is such a hot spot has to do with geography. Warm, moist air from the Gulf of Mexico moves northward and crashes into cool, dry air from the Rocky Mountains and Canada. This creates the perfect ingredients for powerful thunderstorms—and sometimes, tornadoes.

Why Here and Not There?: The Science Behind Tornado Hot Spots

So why does Tornado Alley get so many tornadoes, while other parts of the world get very few?

It all comes down to a combination of **flat land**, **air masses**, and **wind patterns**. The central U.S. is mostly wide, flat plains. There are no large mountains to block or slow down weather systems. That means warm and cold air masses can collide more directly, building huge thunderstorms.

Other factors include:

- **Jet Stream**: A powerful high-altitude wind current that flows from west to east. When it dips over the central U.S., it helps create wind shear—an important ingredient for tornadoes.

- **Dry Line**: A boundary where moist air from the Gulf meets dry air from the deserts of the Southwest. This line often triggers severe storms.

- **Storm Energy**: Warm, moist air rises quickly and creates the unstable conditions that can power rotating storms.

While other regions have thunderstorms, they don't usually have this same combination of wind patterns and open geography. That's what makes Tornado Alley unique.

Other Tornado Zones Around the World: From Bangladesh to Australia

Tornadoes don't just happen in the United States. In fact, they've been spotted on every continent except Antarctica. While no country gets as many tornadoes as the U.S., other nations still face dangerous twisters.

Here are some of the world's tornado-prone areas:

- **Bangladesh and Eastern India**: Believe it or not, Bangladesh has some of the deadliest tornadoes in world history. The 1989 Daulatpur–Saturia tornado killed over **1,300 people**.

- **Canada**: Canada ranks second in the world for tornadoes, especially in provinces like Ontario, Alberta, and Manitoba.

- **Argentina and Brazil**: Parts of South America experience strong tornadoes, especially during their spring and summer months.

- **Australia**: Tornadoes happen here too, especially in the southeastern parts of the country. Most are small, but a few have caused serious damage.

- **Europe**: The United Kingdom, Germany, France, and Italy all see tornadoes from time to time. Though usually weaker than U.S. tornadoes, they can still be dangerous.

Many countries don't have the same radar systems and reporting networks that the U.S. has, so some tornadoes go unreported or are mistaken for other types of storms. But tornadoes are a global phenomenon, and no place is completely safe from them.

Seasonal Twisters: When Tornadoes Are Most Common

Tornadoes can happen at any time of year, but they're more common in certain seasons—especially **spring and early summer**. That's when the temperature contrasts between warm and cold air are strongest, fueling storm systems.

In Tornado Alley, the busiest tornado months are:

- **April**
- **May**
- **June**

During these months, the sun warms the land quickly, while cool air still lingers above. This sets the stage for powerful thunderstorms. May is usually the peak month for tornado activity in the central U.S.

But tornado seasons vary by region:

- **Southern U.S. (like Texas and Alabama)**: Tornado season starts earlier, often in **March or April**.
- **Northern U.S. (like Minnesota or the Dakotas)**: Tornadoes come later, usually in **June or July**.
- **Florida**: Has two peaks—one in the spring and another during **hurricane season** in late summer and early fall.

In the Southern Hemisphere, tornado season is flipped—occurring in **October to January**, during their spring and summer months.

Tornadoes have even occurred in **winter**, though they're much less common. Still, meteorologists stay on alert year-round, just in case.

Mapping Tornado Paths: Famous Tornado Routes Across History

Some tornadoes are so powerful or travel so far that they earn a place in weather history. By studying their paths, scientists can better understand how and where tornadoes move—and how to keep people safe.

Here are a few of the most famous tornado tracks:

- **The Tri-State Tornado (1925)**: This tornado holds the record for the longest path—**219 miles** through Missouri, Illinois, and Indiana. It killed 695 people and destroyed entire towns.
- **Joplin, Missouri (2011)**: An EF5 tornado tore through the city, causing massive destruction along a path nearly **22 miles** long. It remains one of the costliest and deadliest tornadoes in modern U.S. history.
- **El Reno, Oklahoma (2013)**: The widest tornado ever recorded—**2.6 miles wide**. Its path was only about 16 miles, but its immense width made it incredibly dangerous.
- **Tuscaloosa–Birmingham (2011)**: A large EF4 tornado traveled over **80 miles**, hitting both rural and urban areas in Alabama.
- **Andover, Kansas (1991)**: This powerful tornado carved a path over 46 miles, damaging hundreds of homes and becoming one of the most famous tornadoes caught on video.

Tornado paths are unpredictable. Some zigzag, others move in a straight line. Some move quickly, others slowly. Scientists use radar, storm reports, and eyewitness accounts to map these tracks and study patterns. This information helps improve tornado forecasting and early warning systems.

Tornadoes may seem random, but where they happen—and when—follows certain patterns. From the windswept plains of

Tornado Alley to the farmlands of Bangladesh, these mighty storms leave their mark around the globe. By learning where and when tornadoes strike most often, scientists can help communities prepare and stay safe. Next, we'll explore the most famous tornadoes in history—storms so powerful and unforgettable, they changed everything in their paths.

Chapter 5: Famous Tornadoes in History

The Tri-State Tornado (1925): Deadliest in U.S. History

On March 18, 1925, one of the most terrifying tornadoes in American history ripped through the heartland of the country. Known as the **Tri-State Tornado**, this massive twister traveled across **three different states**—Missouri, Illinois, and Indiana—leaving behind an unbelievable trail of destruction.

Here are some astonishing facts about this tornado:

- It lasted over **3 hours**, which is extremely rare for any tornado.
- Its path stretched **219 miles**, the longest continuous tornado track ever recorded.
- It killed **695 people** and injured more than **2,000** others, making it the **deadliest tornado** in U.S. history.

The tornado destroyed entire towns, including **Murphysboro, Illinois**, which suffered the highest death toll from a single tornado in any one community. At the time, there were no warning systems or advanced weather forecasts like we have today, which meant people were caught completely off guard.

Even nearly 100 years later, the Tri-State Tornado remains one of the most studied and talked-about tornadoes in history. It taught scientists a lot about the power of nature—and the need for better weather awareness.

Joplin, Missouri (2011): An EF5 Disaster in Modern Times

On May 22, 2011, the city of **Joplin, Missouri**, experienced one of the most devastating tornadoes in recent memory. This was not a small twister—it was a monstrous **EF5** tornado, the strongest rating possible on the Enhanced Fujita Scale.

Here's what made the Joplin tornado so significant:

- Winds were estimated at **over 200 miles per hour**.
- It caused **161 deaths** and more than **1,000 injuries**.
- The tornado caused **over $2.8 billion** in damage, making it the **costliest tornado in U.S. history**.

The tornado was nearly a mile wide and cut through the center of Joplin, destroying homes, schools, and even a hospital. What made it even more tragic was that it struck during the late afternoon when many people were out shopping or driving home.

Thanks to video footage, news reports, and survivor stories, the Joplin tornado became a powerful example of both the destructive force of tornadoes and the bravery of people helping one another in the aftermath.

Moore, Oklahoma (Multiple Years): A City Repeatedly Struck

If there's one town in America that seems to have a target on its back when it comes to tornadoes, it's **Moore, Oklahoma**. This city, located right in Tornado Alley, has been hit by **multiple powerful tornadoes**, including **two EF5 storms** within just 14 years.

- In **1999**, Moore was struck by a massive EF5 tornado with winds over **300 miles per hour**, the fastest ever recorded on Earth. It caused widespread destruction and 36 deaths.

- In **2013**, another EF5 tornado tore through Moore, killing 24 people and damaging or destroying **over 1,000 homes and buildings**, including schools.

Both tornadoes happened in the month of May, and both received national attention. The 2013 tornado hit during school hours, prompting heroic efforts by teachers to protect students in elementary schools.

Despite the repeated disasters, Moore has continued to rebuild each time, and today it's known for having some of the strictest building codes in the country for tornado safety.

Tuscaloosa–Birmingham Super Outbreak (2011)

In April 2011, a record-breaking outbreak of tornadoes swept across the southeastern United States. One of the most destructive tornadoes during this outbreak struck **Tuscaloosa and Birmingham**, two major cities in **Alabama**, on April 27.

This powerful EF4 tornado caused:

- **Over 60 deaths**
- **More than 1,500 injuries**
- A damage path stretching **80 miles** across Alabama

The tornado was part of a **historic Super Outbreak** that included **more than 360 tornadoes** over several days. It was the **largest tornado outbreak ever recorded in the U.S.**, affecting multiple states and resulting in over **300 fatalities** in total.

The Tuscaloosa-Birmingham tornado flattened entire neighborhoods, threw cars through the air, and left behind a heartbreaking scene of destruction. It proved that even cities—not just rural areas—can be vulnerable to deadly tornadoes.

Other Epic Tornadoes Around the World

While the United States sees the most tornadoes each year, other countries have experienced incredibly powerful and deadly twisters too. Here are a few examples of tornadoes that made history beyond U.S. borders:

- **Daulatpur–Saturia, Bangladesh (1989)**: This tornado is believed to be the **deadliest in world history**, killing **more than 1,300 people**. The storm struck a densely populated area, and many homes were poorly built, making the destruction even worse.

- **Eastern Russia (1984)**: An unusually violent tornado ripped through the city of **Ivanovo**, destroying factories, homes, and schools. It was one of the worst tornadoes ever recorded in Russia, with over **400 injuries** and dozens of deaths.

- **Roanoke, Illinois (2004)**: Though not as deadly, this tornado is remembered for its incredibly **fast formation**—it touched down just minutes after a warning was issued. It destroyed the town's fire station and church but, thankfully, caused no fatalities.

- **New South Wales, Australia (1976)**: An F4 tornado destroyed over 100 homes and killed five people. Tornadoes are rare in Australia, which made this storm especially shocking.

- **South Africa (1999)**: A deadly tornado in the town of **Umtata** killed 25 people and left thousands homeless. It remains one of the worst tornadoes in African history.

Tornadoes may not be as common in some parts of the world, but when they strike, the results can be just as devastating. These storms don't care about borders—they follow the wind, the weather, and the storm systems that create them.

From the deadly Tri-State Tornado to the heartbreaking devastation in Joplin and Moore, tornadoes have left a powerful mark on history. They've reshaped towns, changed lives, and pushed scientists and communities to better prepare for the next storm. In the next chapter, we'll explore the people who chase these storms—on purpose. Get ready to ride along with the brave storm chasers who follow tornadoes up close.

Chapter 6: Chasing the Storm

Who Are Storm Chasers?: Scientists, Filmmakers, Hobbyists

Most people run away from tornadoes—but storm chasers do the opposite. They go out of their way to get *closer* to tornadoes. But why?

There are several different types of storm chasers:

- **Scientists and Meteorologists** chase storms to learn more about how tornadoes form, move, and behave. They use their findings to improve weather forecasting and warning systems.

- **Filmmakers and Photographers** want dramatic, up-close footage and images of tornadoes. Their work is often used in documentaries, news reports, and movies.

- **Hobbyists and Weather Enthusiasts** are passionate about storms and travel across the country just to see tornadoes in person. Some are former scientists or storm lovers who simply enjoy the thrill.

No matter what type of storm chaser they are, they all share one thing in common: a deep respect for the power of nature. Most chasers are careful, well-trained, and work in teams to stay safe while collecting valuable information.

Tools of the Trade: Doppler Radar, Weather Balloons, GPS, and More

Storm chasing isn't just about watching the sky. It requires technology, planning, and teamwork. To stay safe and find tornadoes, chasers use a variety of high-tech tools:

- **Doppler Radar**: This special radar can detect rotation inside thunderstorms. Chasers track radar images on laptops or tablets to figure out where a tornado might form.

- **GPS (Global Positioning System)**: Helps chasers navigate through unfamiliar roads and stay close to the storm's path without getting lost.

- **Weather Balloons**: Some research teams release balloons with instruments that measure temperature, pressure, and wind at different heights.

- **Anemometers**: Devices that measure wind speed. These are sometimes mounted on storm-chasing vehicles.

- **Cameras and Video Equipment**: Used to record tornadoes from a safe distance. High-speed cameras help capture every detail of a spinning funnel.

- **Mobile Weather Stations**: Some vehicles are packed with weather sensors to measure humidity, pressure, and wind on the go.

- **Drones**: More and more chasers are using drones to fly near tornadoes and gather aerial footage and data.

Together, these tools allow storm chasers to do more than just watch—they can collect important scientific data that helps save lives.

Chasing Tornadoes Safely: How Professionals Minimize Risk

Chasing tornadoes may sound exciting, but it's also dangerous. That's why professionals follow strict safety rules to protect themselves and others.

Here are some ways storm chasers stay safe:

- **They never chase alone**. Most chasers work in teams, so there's always someone watching the radar or navigating while the others focus on the storm.

- **They keep a safe distance**. The best view isn't always the closest one. Chasers know how far they can go without putting themselves in danger.

- **They study the roads**. Before a chase, teams look at maps and plan their routes so they won't get trapped by a tornado with no way out.

- **They follow weather warnings**. Even storm chasers pay attention to alerts and watches. If a storm is too risky, they'll back off.

- **They communicate constantly**. Teams use radios, phones, and group chats to keep in touch with each other—and with emergency services, if needed.

Unfortunately, some people ignore safety rules and take unnecessary risks. Real storm chasers know that safety comes first, and that no photo or video is worth a life.

What They've Learned: Scientific Discoveries from Chasing Storms

Storm chasers have helped scientists learn more about tornadoes than ever before. Thanks to the data they've gathered, we now know:

- **How tornadoes form**: By placing instruments inside storms, scientists can better understand the exact moment when a funnel cloud becomes a tornado.

- **What causes tornadoes to strengthen or weaken**: Chasers have collected data on how changes in air pressure, temperature, and wind affect a tornado's power.

- **How tornadoes move**: Watching tornadoes up close has helped researchers improve prediction models and warning times.

- **What kind of debris tornadoes pick up**: By tracking the size and type of debris, scientists can estimate a tornado's strength more accurately.

One of the biggest breakthroughs came from a project called **VORTEX (Verification of the Origins of Rotation in Tornadoes Experiment)**. In this study, storm chasers worked with scientists to study tornado formation in real time using mobile radars, weather sensors, and tracking vehicles. Their work helped improve tornado warning systems and saved lives.

A Day in the Life of a Storm Chaser: Real-Life Examples Kids Can Follow

Ever wonder what it's like to be a storm chaser for a day? It's not just racing through the plains in a cool truck. Here's what a typical chase day might look like:

Morning:

- The team meets early to check weather models, radar, and forecasts.
- They plan their route based on where storms are most likely to form.
- Equipment is loaded and tested—radar units, cameras, laptops, and safety gear.

Afternoon:

- As the sun heats the land, conditions become right for storms.
- The team drives hundreds of miles to the "target area" where they believe tornadoes might form.
- They watch the sky for signs of rotation—wall clouds, dark green skies, and changing winds.

Evening:

- If a tornado forms, they follow it at a safe distance, recording video and collecting data.
- They may report damage or tornado sightings to local emergency services to help keep others safe.
- Once the storm ends or night falls, they regroup, check their equipment, and often sleep in hotels—or even their vehicles.

One famous storm chaser, **Reed Timmer**, has appeared on TV and in documentaries. He uses armored vehicles called "Dominator" trucks to get extremely close to tornadoes. While his chases are exciting, he always emphasizes the importance of safety, planning, and respect for the storm.

Storm chasing isn't just about the thrill—it's about science, safety, and understanding. Thanks to storm chasers, we know more about tornadoes than ever before. These brave men and women help researchers collect crucial data that leads to better forecasts, faster warnings, and safer communities. Now that you've seen how tornadoes are tracked and studied, it's time to learn how we predict them—and what to do when one might be headed your way.

Chapter 7: Tornado Warnings and Watches

What's the Difference?: Watch vs. Warning Explained

When the skies start to darken and storms roll in, it's important to know what different weather alerts mean. Two of the most important tornado alerts are **tornado watch** and **tornado warning**. Even though they sound similar, they mean very different things.

- A **Tornado Watch** means that the conditions are right for tornadoes to form. It doesn't mean one has been spotted yet—it means the ingredients are all there. Think of it like mixing cake batter. You haven't baked a cake yet, but you've got all the pieces ready. During a tornado watch, you should pay close attention to the weather and be ready to act quickly if a warning is issued.

- A **Tornado Warning** means a tornado has been spotted or detected by radar. This is the time to take immediate action—seek shelter right away. Tornado warnings are issued for specific areas and usually last less than an hour. This is when the cake is actually in the oven—and it's about to rise fast.

Understanding the difference between a watch and a warning can save lives. During a watch, be alert. During a warning, get to a safe place.

How Forecasting Works: How Meteorologists Detect Tornadoes

Predicting tornadoes is one of the toughest jobs in weather science. Meteorologists, the scientists who study weather, spend their lives learning how to read the sky and spot danger before it arrives.

Here's how tornado forecasting typically works:

1. **Data Gathering**: Meteorologists collect information from satellites, weather balloons, radar, and ground stations. They look for signs of instability in the atmosphere.

2. **Modeling**: Supercomputers run weather models that predict how storms might develop. These models take into account wind, temperature, pressure, and humidity at many levels in the atmosphere.

3. **Storm Analysis**: When a strong thunderstorm forms, forecasters watch for signs of rotation using Doppler radar. If the radar shows rotation in the storm, they know it may be capable of producing a tornado.

4. **Visual Confirmation**: Spotters on the ground may confirm the presence of a funnel cloud or tornado. That helps meteorologists decide whether to issue a warning.

Because tornadoes can form quickly and without much warning, forecasters must stay alert and act fast when storms begin to rotate.

Technology That Helps Predict Storms: Satellites, Radar, and Weather Stations

Forecasting tornadoes wouldn't be possible without modern technology. Here are some of the amazing tools scientists use to keep us safe:

- **Satellites**: Orbiting high above Earth, satellites take pictures of weather systems from space. They help meteorologists spot the development of large storm systems and track their movement.

- **Doppler Radar**: One of the most important tools for tornado detection, Doppler radar can "see" inside storms. It shows how fast rain and wind are moving, which helps forecasters detect rotation that could lead to a tornado.

- **Weather Balloons**: These are launched into the atmosphere with instruments that measure temperature, humidity, and wind at different altitudes. They help scientists understand the full structure of a storm.

- **Weather Stations**: Scattered across the country, these stations measure wind speed, pressure, temperature, and rainfall. This data gives meteorologists a real-time picture of weather conditions on the ground.

- **Computer Models**: Using powerful computers, scientists run simulations of how the weather might behave. These models help them estimate where and when tornadoes might form.

Thanks to these tools, weather experts can often predict the likelihood of tornadoes hours before storms arrive.

Sirens, Alerts, and Broadcasts: How Warnings Reach the Public

Once a tornado warning is issued, getting the word out quickly is the top priority. Here's how you might learn about a tornado in your area:

- **Outdoor Warning Sirens**: These loud alarms are used in many towns and cities to warn people who are outside. If you hear a tornado siren, take cover right away.

- **TV and Radio Broadcasts**: News stations break into regular programming to give storm updates, including maps, times, and safety instructions.

- **Weather Radios**: These special radios are programmed to turn on automatically when a weather alert is issued. They're useful at night or when the power goes out.

- **Mobile Alerts**: Most smartphones now receive emergency alerts from the National Weather Service. You'll hear a loud tone and see a message telling you where the warning is and what action to take.

- **Apps and Social Media**: Weather apps, like those from The Weather Channel or NOAA, offer real-time updates. Social media also helps people share alerts and storm locations fast.

Even with all this technology, it's important to have a **plan** ahead of time. Know where your safe spot is and act quickly when a warning is issued.

How Fast Can Tornadoes Form?: The Challenge of Early Warning

One of the biggest challenges in tornado forecasting is that some tornadoes form **very quickly**—sometimes in just a few minutes. While meteorologists work hard to give warnings early, there isn't always much time between a funnel cloud forming and a tornado touching down.

Some tornadoes can form with:

- **As little as 5–10 minutes** of warning
- **No visible funnel** until they are already on the ground
- **Rapid intensification**, going from weak to strong in seconds

Because of this, meteorologists aim to improve the speed and accuracy of their warnings. In the past few decades, the average warning time has increased from around 5 minutes to **13–15 minutes**, and in some cases, even **30 minutes**.

Even a few minutes can make a huge difference. That's why storm spotters, radar systems, and fast communication all play a role in keeping people safe. Researchers are always trying to develop better models, faster radars, and more accurate prediction systems to stay one step ahead of the storm.

Knowing the difference between watches and warnings—and understanding how weather scientists predict tornadoes—can help save lives. Whether it's a siren blaring, a phone buzzing, or a meteorologist warning on TV, these alerts are signals to take shelter and stay safe. Up next, we'll dive into how to protect yourself and others when a tornado is on the ground.

Chapter 8: Staying Safe During a Tornado

Where to Go and What to Do: Best and Worst Places to Be

When a tornado warning is issued, the most important thing you can do is take action right away. The faster you get to a safe place, the better your chances of staying safe. But where exactly should you go?

Best Places to Be During a Tornado:

- **Basement or Storm Cellar**: Underground is the safest place to be. Stay away from windows and cover your head.

- **Small, Windowless Interior Room**: If you don't have a basement, go to the lowest floor of your home, like a bathroom or closet in the center of the house.

- **Hallways Away from Windows**: A hallway in the middle of the house can also provide some protection.

- **Storm Shelter or Safe Room**: Some homes, schools, and buildings have specially built safe rooms designed to withstand strong winds.

Worst Places to Be:

- **Mobile Homes**: These are not safe during tornadoes. If you live in one, get to a storm shelter or nearby sturdy building.

- **Under a Bridge or Overpass**: Wind speeds can actually increase in these areas, making them more dangerous.
- **Near Windows**: Flying glass is one of the top causes of tornado-related injuries.
- **Large Open Rooms**: Gymnasiums and cafeterias with wide roofs are not safe during tornadoes.

Always know where your safe spot is—at home, at school, and anywhere else you spend time.

Tornado Drills at School and Home: Why Practice Matters

You may have experienced a tornado drill at school, where you crouch down in a hallway or a safe room, covering your head. These drills aren't just a routine—they're serious practice that can save lives.

Why tornado drills matter:

- **They help you react quickly**. In an emergency, there's no time to think about what to do—you need to act fast.
- **They teach teamwork**. Everyone has a role, whether it's staying quiet, helping a younger student, or following a teacher's lead.

- **They build muscle memory**. Practicing the same steps helps your body know what to do automatically, even when you're scared.

You can also have tornado drills at home. Sit down with your family and make a plan:

- Choose your safe room.
- Practice getting there quickly.
- Assign roles—who grabs the safety kit, who checks on pets, etc.

The more you practice, the more confident and prepared you'll be.

Creating a Tornado Safety Kit: Items Every Family Should Have

Being prepared doesn't just mean knowing where to go—it also means having the right supplies on hand. A **tornado safety kit** helps you stay safe, warm, and informed if you're stuck in your safe spot for a while.

Here's what a good kit should include:

- **Flashlight and Extra Batteries**: Power can go out during storms.

- **Battery-Powered Weather Radio**: To hear updates if cell service goes out.
- **First Aid Kit**: For treating small injuries.
- **Bottled Water and Non-Perishable Snacks**: Enough for everyone for at least a few hours.
- **Blankets or Sleeping Bags**: To stay warm if it's cold.
- **Whistle**: To signal for help if you're trapped.
- **Phone Charger or Battery Bank**: So you can contact help if needed.
- **Personal Items**: Medications, pet supplies, and anything specific to your family's needs.

Store the kit in your designated safe area and check it every few months to make sure everything is still working and not expired.

What If You're Outside?: Tips for Being in a Car, Field, or Campground

Tornadoes don't always strike when you're at home. What if you're at a park, in the car, or camping? It's still possible to stay safe, but you have to act fast and think clearly.

If You're in a Car:

- **Do not try to outrun a tornado** unless it's far away and you have a clear route. Tornadoes can change direction quickly.

- **If possible, drive at a right angle away from the tornado's path**—for example, if the tornado is moving north, drive east or west.

- **If there's no time**, pull over and find a low ditch to lie in, covering your head. Stay far from your car—it could be picked up by the wind.

If You're in a Field or Park:

- **Find a ditch or low-lying area**, lie flat, and cover your head.

- **Stay away from trees**, which can fall or be struck by debris.

- **Watch for flooding** in low spots, which can also be dangerous during storms.

If You're Camping or in a Tent:

- **Get to a sturdy building** if at all possible. Tents and RVs are not safe.

- If there's no building nearby, find a ditch or low area, lie flat, and cover your head with your arms or backpack.

Tornadoes may be unpredictable, but having a plan gives you the best chance of staying safe wherever you are.

Staying Calm and Smart: What Kids Can Do to Help Themselves and Others

Tornadoes can be scary, and it's okay to feel nervous. But staying calm can help you—and the people around you—stay safe.

Here are some smart things kids can do during a tornado emergency:

- **Follow instructions**: Whether at home or school, listen to adults and do what they say quickly.
- **Stay low and quiet**: This helps everyone hear warnings and keeps the group calm.
- **Help younger kids**: Hold hands, share a flashlight, or talk to them to keep them calm.
- **Know your address and emergency contacts**: If you ever get separated, this helps first responders reunite you with your family.
- **Keep your safety kit nearby**: You can help hand out supplies or turn on the radio.

After the storm, be careful of broken glass, downed power lines, or sharp debris. Wait for adults or emergency workers to give the all-clear before leaving your safe spot.

Tornado safety starts long before the storm. By learning where to go, what to bring, and how to stay calm, you become a strong and prepared member of your family and community. In the next chapter, we'll take a look at what happens *after* a tornado passes—how people recover, rebuild, and come together in the aftermath.

Chapter 9: What Happens After a Tornado?

Damage and Debris: What Tornadoes Leave Behind

When a tornado passes through a town or countryside, it doesn't leave things the way it found them. In just a few minutes, a tornado can change the entire landscape. What it leaves behind is often a mix of broken buildings, scattered belongings, and snapped trees—called **debris**.

The kind of damage depends on the tornado's strength. A weak tornado might break windows and knock over fences, while a strong one can:

- Tear roofs off houses
- Flatten buildings
- Uproot large trees
- Flip cars and trucks
- Toss debris for miles

Tornado debris can be made up of almost anything—wood, metal, glass, furniture, clothes, or even things like toys, mailboxes, or trampolines. After the storm, roads might be blocked, power lines could be down, and homes might be unsafe to enter.

Cleanup begins as soon as it's safe, but the first few hours and days are often the hardest. For families, it can feel overwhelming. Everything looks different, and there's a lot of confusion. That's when the community steps in to help.

Helping Hands: Emergency Responders, Volunteers, and Community Heroes

Right after a tornado, one of the most important things people need is **help**—and it usually comes fast. Emergency responders like **firefighters, police officers, paramedics**, and **search-and-rescue teams** arrive quickly to check for injuries, search for trapped people, and begin organizing help.

Many others pitch in too:

- **Volunteers** bring food, water, blankets, and tools to help clean up.
- **Electric workers** fix downed power lines and restore electricity.
- **Doctors and nurses** treat injuries at hospitals or temporary clinics.
- **Church groups, neighbors, and local businesses** often donate supplies or shelter.

Some people even drive in from other towns or states to lend a hand. These community heroes don't wear capes—but their help makes a huge difference. They remind everyone that even after disaster strikes, kindness and teamwork are stronger than any storm.

How Cities Rebuild: Cleanup, Reconstruction, and Support

Once the immediate danger has passed, towns and cities begin the long process of **rebuilding**. This takes weeks, months, or even years, depending on how much was destroyed. It usually happens in phases:

1. **Clearing Debris**: Bulldozers, dump trucks, and volunteers work to remove broken trees, fallen bricks, and shattered glass.

2. **Restoring Power and Water**: Utility crews work hard to fix what was damaged so people can live safely again.

3. **Repairing Roads and Schools**: Schools, libraries, and businesses often need to be rebuilt from the ground up.

4. **Helping Families Recover**: Local governments, insurance companies, and disaster-relief organizations provide money, supplies, and temporary housing for those who lost everything.

Organizations like the **Red Cross** and **FEMA (Federal Emergency Management Agency)** provide assistance, while towns may hold community meetings to plan rebuilding efforts.

In many places, homes are rebuilt stronger, with safer rooms or better materials to help protect against future storms. Parks are replanted, businesses reopen, and over time, things begin to look like home again.

Emotional Recovery: How People Deal with Fear and Loss

While buildings can be rebuilt, **emotional healing** can take longer. Tornadoes often leave people feeling scared, sad, or confused—especially if they lost their home, their pets, or someone they love.

Kids might:

- Have trouble sleeping or have bad dreams
- Be afraid of storms, loud noises, or even the dark
- Feel anxious about being separated from family members

It's completely normal to feel this way after something frightening. Talking about your feelings with parents, teachers, or counselors can help. Drawing pictures, writing stories, or playing with friends are also ways to cope.

Many communities offer **support groups** or counseling after a disaster, so kids and adults can talk about what happened and learn how to feel safe again.

Even if things look different after a tornado, with time and love, families and neighborhoods can grow stronger. Being together and supporting one another is the heart of recovery.

Nature's Comeback: How Animals and Plants Return After Destruction

Believe it or not, nature is pretty good at **bouncing back** after a tornado. Though the landscape may look bare at first, signs of life return sooner than you might think.

- **Birds** often return within days, perching on broken branches or new fence posts.
- **Insects** like butterflies and bees begin buzzing around once flowers regrow.
- **Grass and trees** slowly recover, especially with sunshine and rain.
- **Squirrels, rabbits, and deer** find new places to live, often in areas that were only slightly damaged.

People sometimes help speed up nature's recovery by planting trees, laying new grass, or building animal shelters. Over time, green returns, flowers bloom again, and the scars left by the storm begin to fade.

In some cases, new growth appears where none existed before. That's one of the amazing things about nature—it's resilient. It doesn't give up, and it always finds a way to grow again.

What comes after a tornado can be tough, but it's also a time when people come together, support each other, and show strength. From helping neighbors and rebuilding homes to watching the first tree sprout again, recovery is possible—and inspiring. In the next chapter, we'll clear up some of the most common tornado myths and uncover the truth behind the twister tales you may have heard.

Chapter 10: Tornado Myths Busted

"Open the Windows!": Debunking This and Other Home Myths

For many years, people believed that if a tornado was coming, the best thing to do was to **open the windows** in your house. The idea was that the tornado would create a drop in air pressure outside, and opening the windows would equalize the pressure and prevent the house from exploding. Sounds reasonable, right?

Wrong.

This myth has been proven false by modern science and storm damage research. Here's why:

- **Opening windows wastes time** you could be using to get to safety.

- **Tornado winds break windows anyway**, usually before pressure could build up.

- **It's the wind and flying debris**, not pressure, that does the most damage to homes.

In fact, opening windows might make things worse by allowing debris and wind to rush into your house. The best thing you can do when a tornado is coming? **Leave the windows alone** and head straight to your designated safe spot.

"Tornadoes Can't Hit Cities": Truth About Urban Tornado Strikes

Some people believe tornadoes only strike open fields and farms—and that **cities are protected** somehow. That's not true. While it's **less common** for a tornado to hit a major city (mostly because cities cover smaller areas compared to rural land), it can and **does** happen.

Here are a few real examples of tornadoes hitting urban areas:

- In **1999**, a tornado hit **downtown Salt Lake City**, Utah.
- In **2011**, the EF5 tornado that struck **Joplin, Missouri** destroyed homes, schools, and a hospital.
- The **2013 tornado in Moore, Oklahoma** tore through neighborhoods and reached the city's limits.
- In **2000**, a tornado damaged parts of **downtown Fort Worth, Texas**.

Buildings and pavement don't stop a tornado. If a storm is strong enough and the conditions are right, a tornado will hit wherever it travels—whether it's farmland, a forest, or a big city downtown.

"Highways Are Safe Spots": Why That's Dangerous

When people are caught driving during a tornado, they sometimes think that pulling over and taking shelter **under a**

highway overpass is a good idea. After all, it looks like a strong, sturdy structure, right?

But taking shelter under a bridge or overpass is actually **very dangerous** during a tornado. Here's why:

- Wind speeds can **increase** as they funnel through tight spaces like overpasses.
- Flying debris can bounce off the concrete and injure anyone underneath.
- There's little room to lie flat or stay low, making you more exposed.

If you're driving and can't get to a sturdy building, the safest options are:

- **Drive away from the tornado's path** if it's far enough and the roads are clear.
- **Abandon your car** and lie flat in a ditch or low-lying area, covering your head.

Overpasses may look safe, but in a tornado, they can become wind tunnels—making things even more dangerous.

"The Tornado Skipped My House": What Really Happens

After a tornado strikes, some people say, "It skipped right over us!" This makes it sound like the tornado **jumped into the air** and came back down later. But in most cases, that's **not what's happening**.

Here's the real story:

- Tornadoes **don't usually jump**, but they can **lift off the ground briefly** and then touch back down again.
- Some tornadoes have **narrow paths** and can pass close by without hitting every house in the area.
- The damage might seem random, but it follows the swirling winds inside the funnel. One house may be destroyed while the one next door is barely touched.

So, if it looks like the tornado "skipped" certain spots, it's usually because of how the winds moved—not because the tornado actually hopped through the air.

Where Do These Myths Come From?: Folklore, Old Science, and Pop Culture

Many tornado myths come from a time when people didn't have radar, satellites, or modern weather forecasting. Without science, people tried to explain storms in other ways—often using **folklore**, **guesses**, or even **superstition**.

Some common sources of tornado myths include:

- **Old Wives' Tales**: Stories passed down through generations, like the window myth or beliefs that tornadoes won't cross rivers.

- **Pop Culture**: Movies and TV shows sometimes stretch the truth. Films like *Twister* are exciting, but they're not always accurate.

- **Misunderstood Science**: In the early days of tornado research, even scientists believed some of these myths. But as technology improved, those ideas were replaced with real data.

- **Eyewitness Accounts**: People who experience tornadoes sometimes describe what they *think* happened, even if they couldn't see clearly or were confused during the storm.

That's why science and education are so important. The more we learn about tornadoes, the better we understand what to do—and what not to believe.

Tornado myths can be confusing, but knowing the truth helps you stay safe. Forget the rumors about open windows, "skipping" tornadoes, and hiding under overpasses. The real facts are much more useful—and way more interesting. Up next, we'll take a closer look at how animals react to tornadoes and the incredible ways nature responds to these powerful storms.

Chapter 11: Animals and Tornadoes

How Animals React: Early Warning Signs from Pets and Wildlife

Long before sirens sound or meteorologists issue warnings, animals can sometimes sense that something is wrong. Many pet owners report that their dogs or cats act strangely before a tornado hits. Wildlife, too, often behave in ways that suggest they're picking up on something humans can't see or hear.

Here are a few common animal behaviors noticed before tornadoes:

- **Dogs may bark, whine, or pace**, seeming nervous or agitated for no clear reason.
- **Cats might hide**, refuse to eat, or act jumpy.
- **Birds often go quiet or fly away suddenly**, even when they usually stick around.
- **Livestock**—like cows or horses—may bunch together or refuse to go into barns.

Scientists believe animals may detect changes in **air pressure**, **vibrations**, and even **low-frequency sounds** that happen before a tornado forms. While not all animals react the same way, many do seem to sense danger before people do.

Observing animals closely during storms can offer helpful clues—but it's never a substitute for real weather alerts or preparation.

Famous Animal Stories: Pets Who Saved Lives During Storms

There are many heartwarming tales of animals that played a role in helping their humans during tornadoes. Sometimes, they warn families to take cover. Other times, they help them survive after the storm has passed.

Here are a few incredible stories:

- In **Oklahoma**, a dog named Bella started barking and pulling on her owner's shirt minutes before a tornado warning was issued. The family listened to her, took cover in a closet, and moments later, the roof of their house was torn off.

- In **Joplin, Missouri**, a cat named Oreo refused to come out from under the bed just before the EF5 tornado struck. The family went back to check on her, only to realize the storm was closer than they thought. They all ended up hiding together in the basement—just in time.

- After a tornado in **Arkansas**, a Labrador retriever was found standing guard over her family's baby, who had been thrown from the house in her crib. The baby was unharmed, and the dog never left her side until rescuers arrived.

These stories show just how loyal and intuitive animals can be, especially in moments of crisis.

Tornado Preparedness for Farms and Zoos

Animals that live on farms or in zoos need special care during tornadoes. Since they can't hide in closets or basements like people, farmers and zookeepers must plan ahead to keep them safe.

On farms, tornado safety includes:

- **Sturdy shelters**: Barns with reinforced walls or underground storm bunkers.
- **Tethering livestock**: In open areas, tying animals down may help prevent them from being blown away.
- **Moving animals inside**: Bringing horses, cows, and other large animals into barns when severe weather is expected.

At zoos, the process is more complex:

- **Emergency drills**: Staff practice what to do with large, dangerous, or exotic animals.
- **Special storm enclosures**: Many zoos have built-in safe areas for animals, especially for those that could panic.
- **Backup systems**: Power generators and extra food/water supplies in case the zoo is damaged or

closed.

Planning ahead helps protect both animals and people who care for them during tornado emergencies.

Do Animals Sense Storms Coming?: What Science Says

The idea that animals can "sense" storms has been around for centuries, but what does science actually say about it?

Here's what researchers have found:

- **Air Pressure Sensitivity**: Animals, especially birds and some mammals, can detect drops in air pressure. This often happens right before a big storm.

- **Sound and Vibrations**: Some animals hear **infrasound**, which are sounds too low for humans to hear. Tornadoes produce these low rumbles before and during their formation.

- **Static Electricity**: Storms change the level of static electricity in the air, and animals with sensitive fur or skin might notice it.

- **Instinct**: Evolution has helped many species develop survival instincts. When the weather feels "off," they take shelter automatically.

While science can't confirm that animals "predict" tornadoes, it's clear they can **detect early warning signs** in their own unique ways. That's why paying attention to their behavior can sometimes provide clues.

How Nature Bounces Back: Wildlife After the Storm

After a tornado passes, the land may look unrecognizable. Trees are torn down, nests are gone, and the quiet hum of nature is replaced by sirens and cleanup crews. But over time, **wildlife returns**—and nature begins to heal.

Here's how it happens:

- **Birds build new nests**, often returning to the same areas where their old ones were lost.
- **Squirrels, raccoons, and foxes** find new shelter in the debris or nearby forests.
- **Insects and pollinators** return once plants begin to grow again.
- **Trees and grass** regrow, especially if seeds were buried in the soil during the storm.

Some animals even benefit from the change. Woodpeckers, for example, love dead trees for making nests and finding bugs to eat. Deer and rabbits may find new clearings with more food and sunlight.

People often help this recovery by planting new trees, cleaning up trash, and protecting wildlife habitats that were affected. In a few months, what once looked like a lifeless space may be buzzing with birds, blooming flowers, and signs of life again.

Animals and nature have their own way of surviving storms, adapting, and healing. Whether it's a loyal dog sounding an alarm or a forest slowly regrowing, life continues—even after the strongest winds have passed. In the next chapter, we'll take a journey to outer space and explore the surprising connections between tornadoes on Earth and the storms on other planets.

Chapter 12: Tornadoes on Other Planets?

Dust Devils on Mars: Twister-Like Storms on the Red Planet

Earth isn't the only place in the solar system where swirling winds happen. On **Mars**, scientists have observed something called **dust devils**—miniature twister-like storms that dance across the Martian surface. They're not quite tornadoes, but they look surprisingly similar.

Dust devils on Mars form when **the sun heats the ground**, warming the thin air above it. That warm air rises quickly, and if the wind conditions are just right, the air begins to spin, forming a narrow, tall column of swirling dust. Sound familiar?

Although Martian dust devils can be huge—some stretching over **several miles tall**—they're not very powerful compared to Earth's tornadoes. The atmosphere on Mars is much thinner, so these dust devils don't carry as much energy or cause much damage.

Still, they're fascinating. NASA's rovers, like **Spirit**, **Opportunity**, and **Perseverance**, have photographed and recorded dust devils moving across the surface. In fact, a dust devil once **cleaned off the solar panels** of the Spirit rover, giving it a surprise power boost!

Other Planetary Storms: Jupiter's Great Red Spot and Saturn's Storms

While Mars has its dust devils, gas giants like **Jupiter** and **Saturn** take storms to a whole new level. These planets are home to some of the most **intense and long-lasting storms** in the entire solar system.

- **Jupiter's Great Red Spot** is a giant, swirling storm larger than **three Earths**. It's been spinning for at least **350 years** and shows no signs of stopping. The winds around the edge of the storm reach up to **430 miles per hour**—much faster than even the strongest tornado on Earth.

- **Saturn** has powerful storms too, including one that was captured in 2010 by the Cassini spacecraft. It wrapped all the way around the planet's northern hemisphere and lasted for **months**. Some of Saturn's storms also feature bright flashes of lightning and deep, swirling clouds.

These giant planet storms aren't tornadoes, but they **share some characteristics**—strong rotation, towering cloud formations, and incredible wind speeds. Scientists study them to better understand how storms work not only on distant planets but also here at home.

What Makes Earth Tornadoes Unique?

While other planets have spinning storms and towering whirlwinds, **true tornadoes like we see on Earth are unique**.

That's because tornadoes need a very specific set of conditions to form—conditions that only Earth currently provides.

Here's what makes Earth's tornadoes special:

- **Liquid Water and Moisture**: Earth has oceans, lakes, and humidity in the air, which helps form thunderstorms that lead to tornadoes.

- **Thick Atmosphere**: Our atmosphere has just the right density to create powerful updrafts and downdrafts—needed for tornado formation.

- **Land and Weather Patterns**: Tornadoes happen most often on large, flat landmasses where warm and cold air collide. Earth's geography supports this better than other planets.

- **Jet Stream and Wind Shear**: Earth has fast-moving winds high in the atmosphere that help generate rotating storms. Without this, tornadoes don't form.

In short, while other planets have **stormy weather**, Earth is the only one we know of with the right ingredients for tornadoes like those that touch down in Tornado Alley.

Can We Study Space Storms Like Tornadoes?

Even though space storms are far away, scientists are able to study them using powerful **telescopes**, **space probes**, and **satellites**. These tools send back images and data that help scientists learn more about weather in space.

For example:

- **The Hubble Space Telescope** has taken detailed images of Jupiter's Great Red Spot and watched how it changes over time.

- **NASA's Cassini mission** orbited Saturn and sent back amazing pictures and information about its giant storms.

- **Mars rovers and orbiters** have tracked dust devils from both the surface and space, showing how often and where they appear.

Studying these storms helps scientists understand how **air moves**, how **storms form and grow**, and what weather might be like on other planets—or even on future space colonies. Some researchers also use what they learn about space storms to improve **weather prediction models** here on Earth.

Even though we can't chase a Martian dust devil or fly into Jupiter's storms (yet!), we can still learn a lot by observing them from afar.

Fun Space Twister Facts

Space storms are full of surprises! Here are some amazing facts to blow your mind:

- A dust devil on Mars can be over **five miles tall**, but it would barely ruffle your hair because the Martian atmosphere is so thin.

- Jupiter's Great Red Spot has been swirling for over **three centuries**—longer than the United States has been a country.
- A single storm on Saturn in 2010 was **so large**, it wrapped around the entire planet like a stormy belt.
- Scientists have observed **lightning storms** on Jupiter that are **1,000 times stronger** than those on Earth.
- Even **Venus**, with its thick, toxic atmosphere, experiences giant swirling storms near its poles.

So while Earth's tornadoes are powerful and dangerous, they're part of a much bigger story—one of wild, whirling weather that reaches all the way into outer space.

Tornadoes might be a product of Earth's special atmosphere, but storms are truly **universal**. Whether it's a dust devil on Mars or a centuries-old vortex on Jupiter, swirling weather systems are found across the solar system—and each one helps scientists understand the power of nature just a little better. In the next chapter, we'll return to Earth and discover how humans are building stronger shelters and designing structures to stand up to these powerful storms.

Chapter 13: Building to Survive

Tornado-Proofing Homes: Safe Rooms, Basements, and Bunkers

When it comes to surviving a tornado, where you take shelter can make all the difference. While there's no such thing as a completely "tornado-proof" home, there are smart ways to **design and build houses** that offer much better protection.

One of the most important features is a **safe room**. These specially built rooms are designed to withstand extreme winds and flying debris. Safe rooms:

- Are made with **reinforced concrete, steel, or impact-resistant materials**
- Have **no windows**
- Are built on a **solid foundation**, often inside a garage or central part of the house
- Can be **above or below ground**

Many families also rely on **basements** or **bunkers**. A basement provides natural protection underground, away from dangerous winds. Some people even build storm bunkers in their backyards or under garages, stocked with food, water, and emergency supplies.

Even without a full safe room, choosing an **interior room**—like a bathroom or closet on the lowest floor of your house—can make a big difference during a tornado.

Stronger Materials: Engineering Against the Wind

In tornado-prone areas, building stronger isn't just smart—it's essential. Engineers and architects have developed materials and construction methods to help homes and buildings stand up better to high winds.

Some common improvements include:

- **Impact-resistant windows**: These can handle flying debris better than regular glass.
- **Hurricane ties and clips**: Metal connectors that help hold roofs and walls together during strong winds.
- **Reinforced doors**: Especially on garages, which are often the first part of a home to collapse in a tornado.
- **Concrete walls or insulated concrete forms (ICFs)**: These materials are much tougher than wood or drywall.

Builders are learning from tornado damage. After major storms, experts inspect how and why buildings failed—and then adjust future designs to make them safer. These changes might cost a bit more up front, but they can save homes—and lives—down the road.

How Schools and Hospitals Stay Safe

When tornadoes strike during school or hospital hours, **many lives are at risk**, so these buildings are often equipped with **extra safety features**. Since they care for large groups of people, they have to be ready for anything.

In **schools**, tornado safety includes:

- **Designated tornado-safe zones**, usually interior hallways or windowless classrooms.
- **Reinforced gymnasiums or storm shelters**, especially in newer schools.
- **Emergency drills**, so students and staff know where to go quickly.

In **hospitals**, planning is even more detailed. They often include:

- **Underground or reinforced wings** for patients who can't be moved easily.
- **Backup power systems** to keep critical machines running.
- **Evacuation procedures** for moving patients to safer parts of the building.

Some newer public buildings, especially in tornado-prone regions, are built with **safe rooms large enough to hold hundreds of people**. These structures follow strict building codes set by FEMA and other safety organizations.

The Rise of Tornado Shelters: From Underground to Mobile

Not everyone has a basement, especially in parts of the country with high water tables or rocky soil. That's why more families and communities are turning to **storm shelters**—secure places designed specifically to protect people during tornadoes.

There are different types of tornado shelters:

- **Underground Shelters**: Buried in the ground, often in the backyard or garage. These offer the best protection but may be harder to access if debris blocks the door.

- **Above-Ground Shelters**: Built inside homes or garages, using reinforced steel or concrete. These are easier to enter quickly.

- **Community Shelters**: Found in schools, churches, and mobile home parks. They're built to hold large groups during emergencies.

- **Mobile Shelters**: Some companies now offer pre-built shelters that can be delivered and anchored on a property. These are popular in areas without basements.

Many states offer **grants or tax breaks** for families that install tornado shelters, making it easier for people to invest in safety.

Future Tech in Construction: Smart Buildings and Wind-Resistant Designs

As technology advances, so does the way we build. Engineers and architects are working on **next-generation homes and buildings** that use smart features and innovative designs to stand up better to storms—including tornadoes.

Here are some of the newest ideas:

- **Smart sensors** that detect pressure changes or vibrations and alert homeowners when a storm is nearby.
- **Automated storm shutters** that close over windows at the touch of a button—or automatically during warnings.
- **Modular safe rooms** that can be installed in closets or bedrooms, offering immediate protection.
- **Flexible structures** that bend slightly in strong winds without breaking.
- **Wind tunnel testing** for homes, allowing designers to test buildings against simulated storm conditions.

Even entire neighborhoods are being planned with tornado safety in mind, including underground shelters, strong community centers, and reinforced homes. In the future, tornado-resistant communities could become the new normal in storm-prone areas.

Humans can't stop tornadoes—but we can get smarter about how we live with them. From safe rooms in homes to smart materials and storm shelters, building to survive is all about preparation, science, and a commitment to protecting lives. In the next chapter, we'll meet some people who choose to face these storms head-on: the amateur storm chasers who follow tornadoes for the thrill, the science, and the adventure.

Chapter 14: Tornadoes in Movies, Media, and Pop Culture

Big Twisters on the Big Screen: Tornadoes in Movies

Tornadoes are so powerful and dramatic that they've become a favorite topic for movies—especially action-packed ones! In films, tornadoes are often shown as enormous, fast, and full of danger. While these movies can be exciting, they don't always show tornadoes exactly how they behave in real life.

One of the most famous tornado movies ever made is ***Twister*** (1996). In this film, a team of scientists chases dangerous tornadoes to try to learn more about them. The movie shows:

- Giant, roaring tornadoes forming suddenly
- Flying debris like tractors and cows
- People getting very close to tornadoes without being hurt

Twister helped make tornado science popular and even inspired many real-life meteorologists to start studying storms. While it gets some things right—like the equipment storm chasers use—it also includes exaggerated scenes for entertainment. For example, people can't really hold onto pipes and survive being inside a tornado!

Other movies that feature tornadoes include:

- ***The Wizard of Oz*** (1939): One of the most famous tornado scenes of all time. A twister picks up Dorothy's house and drops it in the magical land of Oz.

- ***Into the Storm*** (2014): A newer movie that shows several tornadoes hitting a town, including a gigantic "firenado"—a fire-filled tornado that really can happen in rare cases.

- ***Night of the Twisters*** (1996): A made-for-TV movie based on a book, following a boy and his family during a tornado outbreak.

While movies often make tornadoes look even more dramatic than they really are, they've played a big part in teaching people about the danger—and wonder—of these storms.

Tornadoes on TV: Documentaries and Weather Specials

Besides movies, tornadoes are also featured in many **TV shows and documentaries** that are more focused on science than storytelling.

Popular tornado documentaries include:

- ***Storm Chasers*** (Discovery Channel): A reality series following real storm chasing teams as they track tornadoes across the U.S. They use special vehicles, radar systems, and cameras to get as close as possible.

- ***NOVA: Deadliest Tornadoes*** (PBS): This program explores how scientists study tornadoes and how communities recover after powerful storms.

- ***Tornado Alley*** (IMAX/National Geographic): A film made for science museums and theaters, showing amazing up-close footage of tornadoes.

These programs help explain the science behind tornadoes and show how real people respond when one is coming. Unlike Hollywood films, these shows focus more on facts and real-world safety.

Even news broadcasts and weather channels often feature **tornado specials**, especially during storm season. These segments might show radar footage, storm chaser videos, or interviews with people who lived through a tornado.

Tornadoes in Books and Stories

Tornadoes have been a part of books and storytelling for a long time—especially in stories set in the Midwest or Tornado Alley. These powerful storms are often used to symbolize change, fear, or exciting adventure.

Some popular tornado-themed books for kids and teens include:

- ***Night of the Twisters*** by Ivy Ruckman: A fictional story inspired by a real tornado outbreak in Nebraska. It follows a young boy and his family trying to survive multiple tornadoes in one night.

- ***Twisters and Other Terrible Storms*** by Mary Pope Osborne and Will Osborne: Part of the Magic Tree House Fact Tracker series, this book explains the science of tornadoes in kid-friendly language.

- ***The Storm Book*** by Charlotte Zolotow: A gentle picture book that explores a storm from a child's point of view—less scary but still powerful.

Tornadoes also appear in **folktales and legends**, especially in places like Kansas, Oklahoma, and Texas where storms are part of everyday life. Some Native American stories describe great winds as spirits, while old pioneer tales often included stories of houses vanishing in twisters.

Tornadoes in Music, Games, and Cartoons

Believe it or not, tornadoes even show up in music, video games, and cartoons!

In **music**, tornadoes are sometimes used as symbols for chaos, love, or life spinning out of control. Country songs, in particular, often mention storms and tornadoes as part of life in rural America.

In **video games**, tornadoes can be part of the challenge:

- In ***The Legend of Zelda*** series, tornadoes sometimes transport the player or act as magical forces.

- In **simulation games** like *SimCity*, tornadoes can randomly appear and cause destruction that players must clean up.

- In racing games, some tornado-themed levels have players dodging flying debris or navigating through wind tunnels.

Cartoons often show tornadoes in silly or exaggerated ways. Characters might get spun around like a top, carried to another land, or comically wrapped around a tree. While these scenes are usually funny, they're very different from what tornadoes do in real life.

What Media Gets Right—and What It Gets Wrong

While tornadoes in movies and shows can be entertaining, it's important to know that **not everything you see is true**. Here's a breakdown:

What media gets right:

- Tornadoes can form quickly and cause massive destruction.
- Storm chasers really do use radar, maps, and armored vehicles.
- The sky often turns greenish before a tornado.

What media gets wrong:

- Tornadoes rarely pick up people and gently set them down elsewhere (like in *The Wizard of Oz*).

- It's not safe to chase tornadoes without training and proper equipment.

- Most tornadoes are **not** massive EF5s. In fact, many are EF0 or EF1 and last only a few minutes.

Media is great for getting people interested in tornadoes, but it's always good to follow up with real science from trusted sources like the National Weather Service or NOAA.

From heart-pounding movie scenes to science-packed documentaries, tornadoes have spun their way into entertainment and education around the world. Whether they're real or imagined, these mighty storms continue to capture the imagination of storytellers, scientists, and kids alike. In the next chapter, we'll travel back in time to see how tornado science began—and how our understanding has grown over the years.

Chapter 15: Become a Tornado Expert

Tornado Vocabulary: Important Words Every Twister Fan Should Know

If you want to speak like a tornado expert, you'll need to know the right words. Meteorologists and storm chasers use specific vocabulary to describe tornadoes, how they form, and what they do. Here are some key terms every tornado enthusiast should know:

- **Funnel Cloud** – A rotating cone-shaped cloud that hasn't touched the ground. Once it does, it becomes a tornado.

- **Vortex** – The spinning motion of air in a tornado or storm.

- **Updraft** – A rising column of warm air that feeds a thunderstorm.

- **Downdraft** – A descending column of cooler air, often bringing rain or hail.

- **Wind Shear** – A change in wind speed or direction with height; an important factor in tornado formation.

- **Supercell** – A powerful type of thunderstorm with a rotating center that can produce tornadoes.

- **EF Scale (Enhanced Fujita Scale)** – The system used to rate tornadoes from EF0 to EF5 based on damage and estimated wind speed.

- **Watch** – A weather alert that means tornadoes *could* form in the area.

- **Warning** – A weather alert that means a tornado has been spotted or detected by radar and people should take cover immediately.

- **Debris Cloud** – The swirl of dust, dirt, and broken objects picked up by a tornado near the ground.

Knowing these terms not only helps you understand how tornadoes work—it also prepares you to explain them to others!

DIY Weather Projects: Tornado-in-a-Bottle, Cloud in a Jar, Wind Tester

Want to learn about tornadoes by doing? Here are a few fun and simple **science projects** you can try at home or in the classroom. They'll help you see weather in action!

1. Tornado-in-a-Bottle

- **What you need**: Two clear plastic bottles, water, duct tape, and glitter (optional).

- **How it works**: Fill one bottle almost full with water. Attach the second bottle on top using duct tape, creating a tight seal. Flip the bottles and swirl the water in a circle. A mini tornado forms inside as the water spins downward!

2. Cloud in a Jar

- **What you need**: A clear jar, hot water, ice, and hairspray.
- **How it works**: Fill the jar with a little hot water, then spray a quick puff of hairspray inside. Place a lid with ice on top. After a few seconds, a cloud will form inside the jar as the warm air meets the cold.

3. Wind Tester

- **What you need**: A pencil with an eraser, a straight pin, a plastic straw, and a paper triangle and tail.
- **How it works**: Make a wind vane by pinning the straw to the pencil eraser so it spins freely. Attach the triangle to one end of the straw and a larger paper tail to the other. Place it outside on a windy day to see which way the wind is blowing.

These activities help you understand the forces that cause wind, storms, and tornadoes—plus, they're fun to build and test!

Books, Videos, and Apps: Where to Learn More

The more you explore, the more you'll understand tornadoes. There are many great books, videos, and apps made just for kids who love weather.

Books:

- *National Geographic Kids: Everything Weather* – Packed with cool photos and facts.

- *Twisters and Other Terrible Storms* – A nonfiction companion to the Magic Tree House books.

- *I Survived the Joplin Tornado, 2011* by Lauren Tarshis – A fictional story based on real events.

Videos and Documentaries:

- *PBS NOVA: Deadliest Tornadoes* – A scientific look at storm tracking.

- *Storm Chasers* (Discovery Channel) – Follows real scientists chasing tornadoes across the Plains.

- National Weather Service and NOAA websites – Great for real-time weather videos and radar.

Apps and Websites:

- *MyRadar* – Shows live weather radar and is easy to use.

- *WeatherBug* or *The Weather Channel* app – Get alerts, forecasts, and maps.

- *NOAA Weather Radio* – Real alerts from the National Weather Service.

Exploring these resources will grow your knowledge and keep you up to date on weather around the world.

How You Can Help During Storm Season: Community and School Roles

Even if you're a kid, there are ways you can make a difference during storm season. Being prepared and helping others makes you a valuable part of your community.

Here's how you can get involved:

- **Learn your school's safety plan**: Know where to go during a drill and help remind classmates.
- **Make an emergency kit with your family**: Gather flashlights, a radio, snacks, and supplies.
- **Create a tornado safety poster**: Hang it at school or in your home to teach others.
- **Help younger siblings during storms**: Show them where to go and help keep them calm.
- **Join or start a Weather Club**: Work with teachers or classmates to learn more and share knowledge.

Being aware, helping others, and staying calm are all signs of a tornado expert in the making.

Tornado Trivia Challenge: Fun Quiz to Test Your Knowledge

Ready to prove how much you've learned? Try answering these trivia questions (answers below—no peeking!):

1. What's the name of the scale used to rate tornado strength?
2. Which U.S. state gets the most tornadoes each year?
3. What does a tornado "watch" mean?
4. What do we call the part of the storm that starts to spin before a tornado forms?
5. Can tornadoes happen on other planets?

Answers:

1. Enhanced Fujita Scale (EF Scale)
2. Texas
3. Conditions are right for tornadoes to form
4. A funnel cloud
5. Yes—dust devils on Mars and giant storms on Jupiter!

Tornadoes are powerful, fascinating, and a little mysterious—but now that you've learned so much, you're well on your way to becoming a true tornado expert! Whether you're building weather projects, spotting funnel clouds on radar, or helping others stay safe, your knowledge can make a real difference. Stay curious, stay safe, and keep watching the skies!

Printed in Dunstable, United Kingdom

71987677R10057